A Simple Gu

Mac

Samuel Harris

The Mac is a powerful system, but as with all computers it's initial complexity can be daunting. However, the Mac is actually a very friendly and easy to use computer, and this book is your guided tour...

Table of Contents

Getting Started

Just as you would do when meeting a new person, when you buy a new Mac you'll need to introduce yourself, and tell it a bit about who you are and what you like!

After plugging in your Mac and any peripherals (as described in the instructions that came with your Mac), press the power button. You will hear a chime, and a grey Apple logo will appear onscreen for a few seconds, followed by a window with some questions for you to answer about yourself, where you come from, and your preferences.

First, you will be asked about your location. Simply use your mouse or trackpad to move the onscreen cursor, and click on your current location in the list below the map of the world. Now, click the 'Continue' button at the bottom of the window.

You'll next be asked which layout your keyboard has. Select the correct layout from the list. If you're unsure which layout your keyboard has, it's most likely that it simply matches the nationality of where you live. For instance, if you live in the UK, pick 'British'. Now, click the 'Continue' button again.

You'll now be asked if you would like to transfer information, such as files, settings, and applications, from another computer to your new Mac. If you do, click the option from the list that matches your needs, and follow the onscreen instructions. If you have no information to transfer, click 'Not Now'. Then, click the 'Continue' button.

The next section asks whether or not to switch on Location Services. This is a feature of OS X that allows your Mac to determine it's geographic location, and share this information with applications that request it. This could be useful, for instance, in a weather forecasting app - instead of having to ask you directly where you live, the app would be able to find out for itself. You will be asked for permission each time an individual app wants to use your location for the first time. If you are comfortable with this, click the checkbox next to the words "Enable Location Services on this Mac" to place a tick in it. If not, leave the box blank. Now, click the 'Continue' button.

Now you'll be asked to enter your Apple ID and password. If you've ever purchased a product from the Apple Online Store, downloaded something from the iTunes store, or bought an app from the App Store, you've used an Apple ID. Sign in with this same username and password here. If you don't think you have an Apple ID, click the 'Create a Free Apple ID' button. Once you've entered your Apple ID, click the 'Continue' button.

You're now asked to agree to Terms and Conditions. Read the terms, and if you agree, click the 'Agree' button at the bottom of the screen. You'll be asked to confirm that you have read the terms, and agree with them; click the 'Agree' button again.

Your Mac can use the Apple ID you signed in with to synchronise all of your Apple devices with each other using a free Apple service called iCloud. We'll talk about iCloud in more depth later in this book, but for now if you have more than one Apple Device you're probably going to want to tick the checkbox next to the words "Set up iCloud on this Mac". If you're not sure, leave the box blank - I'll show you how to switch it on if you change your mind later in the book. Then click the 'Continue' button. If you chose to enable iCloud you'll also have to click the 'Continue' button in the dialogue box that opens.

If you enabled iCloud, the next screen asks whether you'd like to use Find My Mac. Find My Mac allows you to locate your Mac on a map should it get lost or stolen, helping you get it back. It also allows you to lock it, and even remotely erase its contents. If you would like to use this feature, tick the checkbox next to the words 'Set up Find My Mac on this Mac'. Now click continue. If you chose to enable Find my Mac, you'll also be presented with a dialogue box confirming your decision; click 'Allow'.

Now we come to a screen where we create an account for you. Your Mac is capable of allowing multiple users to each have their own personalised area, called an account. Each account has a user's name and a picture associated with it, allowing it to be selected from a list when Your Mac is switched on. The account holds that user's files and preferences, and can be set up in a way that suits that particular person without affecting the other users of the Mac.

We'll only create your account for now, but others can be created later. Type your full name in the 'Full Name' text field, and a shorter name for yourself in the 'Account Name' text field. For example, if your full name were "Thomas Smith", your account name might be "Tom". Next, type a password in the 'Password' field, and confirm it in the field to the right. Make sure to remember this password; you'll need it quite often. Finally there are two checkboxes, tick the first one to allow your account password to be reset with your Apple ID, and tick the second one if you want to secure your user account by requiring your password to be typed to access it. Then click 'Continue'.

Now we need to tell your Mac what time zone you're in. You may see a checkbox allowing you to let your Mac automatically detect your timezone. If so, tick the checkbox. If not, simply click on your approximate location on the map, then select your closest city from the drop-down list by clicking the arrow button in the list box, and then clicking on your closest city. Now click 'Continue'.

Your Mac has almost finished getting to know you now! The final screen asks us to register your new Mac with Apple, which you can do by clicking 'Continue' or skip by clicking 'Skip', before thanking us and presenting the button we've been waiting for: 'Start using your Mac'. Click it, and we can do just that!

The Dock, and Launchpad

The dock is the bar of icons that sits at the bottom of the screen on your Mac, separated into two sections by a line. Think of it as a shortcut bar — the left hand side is a shortcut area for applications (or 'apps' for short), while the right hand side is for files and folders, along with the trash.

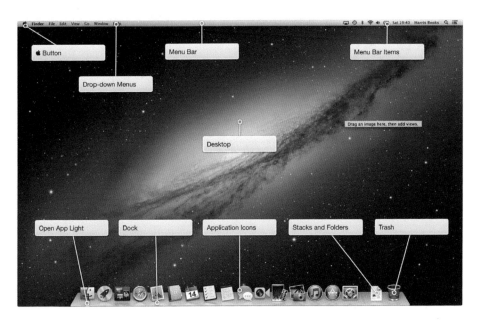

Every application on your Mac can be found in an area called Launchpad - you can get there by clicking on the Icon in your dock that looks like a rocket. Here you will see an onscreen grid that contains all the applications installed on your Mac. However, you don't really want to have to search through all these application icons every time you want to launch your favourite app, and this is where the dock comes in handy. Simply click and drag the icon of each app you think you will use often down onto the left side of the dock, and a shortcut to it will stay there for your convenience. You can also move the icons in both the dock and Launchpad into whatever order you like by dragging them around.

When an app icon in the dock is clicked, it will start to bounce, and the app will open. A small light appears under the icon to signify that it is running. If you wish to quit an app, you can do so by clicking and holding (or right clicking) on the icon, and selecting 'quit'. Occasionally however, an app may stop responding and not be able to quit. If this is the case, wait a minute or so. More often than not the app is simply busy doing something, and will soon become responsive again. If the app is still unresponsive after you have waited however, you can force it to quit by holding the option key (also known as the alt key) as you click the quit option, changing it to 'force quit'. This should close the app immediately.

The right hand side of the dock can hold files and folders. Folders dragged to the right hand side of the dock become 'stacks' — simply a useful way to quickly view files and folders in the dock.

Two stacks are in the dock by default when you buy your Mac: documents, and downloads. Simply drag more files and folders to the dock to create more stacks. Right clicking on a stack gives you options on how to display it, and how to sort it. You may find that the fan view is good for folders with just a few items in them, whereas the grid view is better for folders with many items.

The right hand side of the dock has another purpose. If you have a window open, but don't need it right now and want a place to put it so that it's out of the way, you can shrink it down to an icon in the dock. You can do this by use of the controls in the top left corner of each window. The red button closes the window, the

amber button minimises it to the dock, and the green button resizes the window to fit the content displayed in it.

Settings for the dock itself can be found in System Preferences, but some are also available by right clicking on the line that separates the left and right hand sides of the dock. You can also adjust the size of the dock by dragging this line up or down to make the dock icons bigger or smaller.

Mission Control

Safari, Mail, iTunes, Pages...quite often you can find yourself with many applications open at once, and with these applications comes a sea of open windows to sort through. But there is a better way to get to the window you want than by shuffling through windows to get to what's behind.

It's called Mission Control, and it's very simple, and very elegant. You'll find a dedicated button for Mission Control on the top row of your keyboard - a key with a picture of three rectangles (and F3 written in the corner). You can also access it by clicking the icon labelled 'Mission Control' in your dock (and by using the Multi-Touch gesture discussed later in the book).

What this does is separate all open windows into a grid, so that you can quickly and easily find what you're looking for, and switch to that window. But Mission Control goes far beyond this.

OS X allows you to create additional desktop workspaces. Perhaps you would like an area for work, an area for games, and an area for social networking, but want to keep these separate to avoid having too many windows on screen at once. Creating additional desktops allows you to do this.

Whilst in Mission Control, move your cursor to the top right corner of the screen. You will see a + icon appear; clicking it creates a new desktop workspace for you to use as you wish. You can even drag open windows between these desktops whilst in Mission Control.

The main area of mission control shows your open application windows from the current desktop, but you will also see an area above this. This area contains any additional desktop workspaces you may have created. Clicking on one takes you to it.

The area at the top is also home to applications which are in full-screen mode. Many applications have a full-screen mode, allowing the app to exist in its own workspace and take up the entire screen.

To put an application into full-screen, look at the top right corner of its window. Apps that have a full screen mode have an icon in this top right corner (as shown in the picture on the opposite page). Simply clicking the icon puts the app into full-screen in its own fresh workspace.

When an app is in full-screen mode, the dock is hidden. Simply move your cursor to the bottom of the screen, and the dock will reappear allowing you to switch applications or go back to Mission Control.

Also shown on the top bar in Mission Control, is Dashboard, and we take a look at that in the next section...

What is Dashboard?

Often, you may find yourself needing a quick snippet of information. Perhaps you need to do a simple calculation, check the weather for tomorrow, look up a word in the dictionary, etc. Perhaps you want this information, but not enough to be bothered with opening the calculator or dictionary applications, or browsing to a weather website. You need Dashboard.

Dashboard is a quick, easy, and unobtrusive way to get such information. It appears, you get what you want at a glance, it disappears. Easy. Think of it as an extra area of your screen that lies just out of sight to the left of your regular workspace. Invoking dashboard slides this area across into view, along with useful little 'widgets' of information.

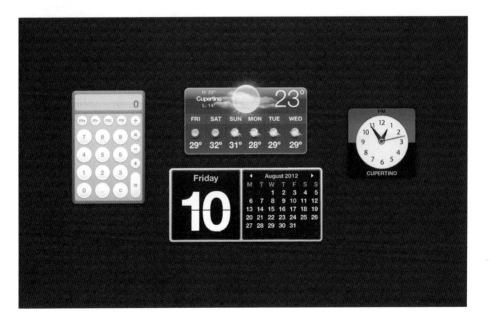

Dashboard can be invoked by clicking the mission control icon in your dock. The far left space at the top is always allocated to Dashboard; simply clicking on its preview takes you to it. You can also access Dashboard by use of the same Multi-Touch gesture you use to access all other desktop workspaces and full screen apps, swiping to the right with four fingers until you reach the leftmost space.

The area that slides into view is the dashboard, complete with four default widgets to get you started — a calculator, a clock, a weather forecast and a calendar. Lets start by setting these up.

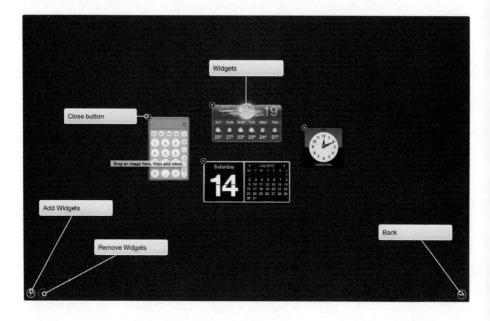

Hover your cursor over the weather widget, and you should see a little 'i' in the bottom right hand corner. Any widgets that have settings have a little 'i' that appears when you hover over it. Click it, and you should see it flip over to reveal settings on its back. Enter your location, or postcode or zip code, and click on the most likely result from the list that appears. Now click done, and the widget should flip back around to show the weather for the location you chose! You can do the same for the clock widget to show whatever time you want to.

This alone is useful, but wouldn't more widgets be even better? Well, look at the bottom left hand corner of your dashboard. See the '+' icon? Click it and you should see icons for even more widgets appear on screen. You can simply click on the icons for the widgets you want, and they will be added to dashboard for you to arrange however you want. You can even have more than one of the same widget at once - useful for seeing the weather or time in more than one location, for instance.

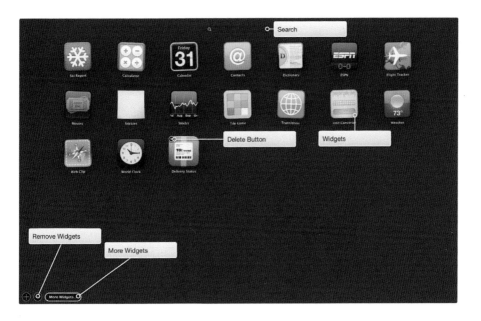

If you find you want more widgets than are built in, click the '+' icon once more, and then click on the button that says 'More Widgets...' in the bottom left corner of the screen. You will be taken to a website where you will find a huge number of widgets to add to your dashboard. Simply find one you want, click 'Download', and the widget should be automatically downloaded, installed, and added to your dashboard.

(Please note, some features and widgets in dashboard require connection to the Internet.)

Multi-Touch your Mac

If you have a modern portable Mac, you may not know that it has a bit of the iPhone and iPad inside of it. The same chip that powers the multi-touch on those devices sits inside your MacBook's trackpad, and your iMac's Magic Mouse or Magic Trackpad, allowing you to use the same multi-touch gestures you're used to using on your iPhone and iPad, on your Mac.

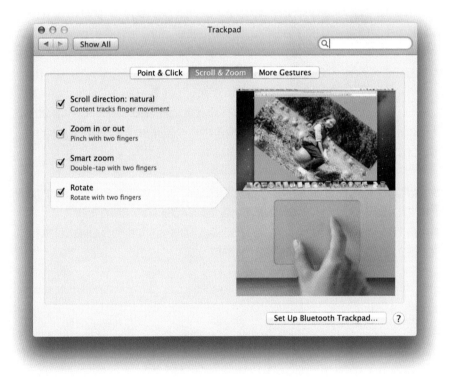

Gestures such as rotating images with two fingers, and pinching to zoom in or zoom out can be performed exactly as on the iPhone and iPad. There are also gestures unique to the Mac, such as two finger scrolling, right clicking by tapping two fingers, and four finger swiping and pinching.

To enable specific gestures, and watch video demonstrations of how each work, go to System Preferences by clicking the Apple logo in the top left of your screen, and choosing 'System Preferences' from the drop-down menu (fourth option down). Then in the window that opens click the 'Trackpad' or 'Mouse' icon, and hover your cursor over each gesture description from each of the three categories to see a video demonstrating it. You can enable or disable each gesture by use of the checkboxes to the left of each gesture description.

Some of these gestures are almost essential, such as right clicking and scrolling. To right click on a trackpad, simply tap it with two fingers. To right click on the Magic Mouse, lift your index finger, and click with your middle finger on the right-hand side of the mouse.

To scroll with a trackpad, place two fingers on the surface of the pad, and move them up to slide the page up, or down to slide the page down. Do the same on the Magic Mouse, but with just one finger.

Stay Organised

OS X includes three great applications to help you stay organised: Calendar, Reminders and Notes.

Calendar

As its name implies, Calendar allows you to store your appointments, and can alert you at a set time when a scheduled appointment's date and time is drawing near. You can also use the application to see your schedule in daily, weekly, monthly and yearly views.

To open Calendar, click its icon in the dock, or in Launchpad if it is not in your dock. At the top of the application you have the day, week, month and year views to choose from - clicking on one of the four tabs switches the calendar to that view.

The easiest way to add an event to your calendar is by clicking the '+' icon in the top left of the window. This opens a small popup text field where you can simply type in what you would like adding to your schedule. For instance, if you are planning on going to see a movie at the cinema at 7pm this Friday, simply type "Movie at 7pm on Friday". Or, if you are going on a business trip next

Thursday and Friday, type "Business Trip next Thursday to Friday". Press the enter key and the event is added to your calendar automatically!

Once the event has been added, the Calendar application pops up a small window, allowing you to check the details of the event, and change or add details if necessary. Details such as the event title, location, date and time can be edited simply by clicking in the appropriate area and typing new details. You can also choose which calendar group the event should be shown in (by default you can choose from Home and Work - home events will appear on your calendar in blue, and work events in green), and set an alert so that the Calendar application will remind you of the event at the time you set. Press the 'Done' button to save any changes you make.

Should you need to edit an event in the future, just double-click on it to bring up the same small popup window once more, and click the 'Edit' button. Enter new details, and click 'Done'. To delete an event, just select the event by clicking on it once, and press the backspace key on your keyboard.

The Reminders application allows you to create lists of 'to-do's, things that you need to do and want to write down as a reminder. The app can then automatically remind you about an item on your list at a set time, or even when you are in a certain location.

To launch the Reminders app, click it's icon in the dock, or from Launchpad if it's not in your dock. The Reminders app consists of two main areas. The left hand side has a column which holds your lists (by default there is just one, named "Reminders"), and the right hand side contains the reminders written in the selected list.

You can use lists as groups for your reminders. You could have a list for the shopping you need to buy, your home reminders, your work reminders, etc. To add a new list, click the '+' icon in the bottom left of the window. A new list is created with the placeholder name "New List". To change the name of the new list, right-click on the list in the left hand column, select 'Rename' from the popup menu, and type a new name.

To add a new reminder to a list, first click on the name of the list you want to add a reminder to in the left hand column. With that list open, click on the '+' icon in the top right of the window. A new, blank reminder is created. Simply type what you want to be reminded about, for instance "Buy Groceries", and press the enter key on your keyboard.

If you would like the app to remind you of an item on your list at a certain time or place, hover your cursor over that item. An 'i' will appear next to the item on the list - clicking it opens a popup window with options for how you would like to be reminded. Click to tick the 'On a Day' checkbox if you would like to be reminded at a specific date and time. Tick the 'At a Location' checkbox if you would like to be reminded when you arrive at or leave a specific location. Then, simply fill in the details of the date and time or location you require, and click 'Done'.

When you have completed an item on a list, click to tick the checkbox next to it to mark it as completed. It will be moved to a new list named 'Completed'.

Notes

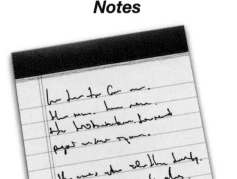

The Notes application is a place to hold any small notes you need to write down, such as notes for a college lecture. To open the Notes app, click it's icon in the dock, or from Launchpad if it's not in your dock.

The Notes app is split into two main sections - on the left hand side is a list of all your notes, while the right hand side displays the contents of the selected note. To create a new note, click the '+' icon in the bottom left of the window. A new blank page of paper will appear in the right hand area. You can now simply type whatever it is you wish to note down. The first line of text you type will become the title of the note shown in the left hand area of the app.

When you have more than one note, simply click on it's title in the list of notes on the left hand side, or if you have many notes you may find it easier to search for the note by typing something in the search field above the list of notes. You can search for any word that is in the title or the note itself.

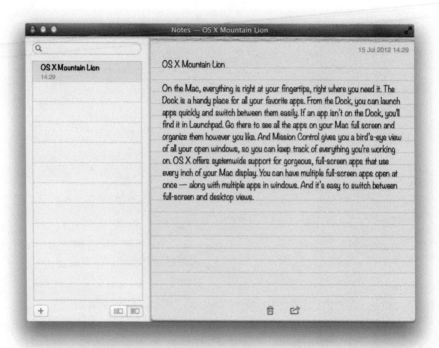

Should you ever wish to delete a note, first select it in the notes list, then click on the icon that looks like a bin or trashcan at the bottom of the note area.

Stay in Sync, with iCloud

You may have heard a lot of talk recently about something called 'Cloud Computing'. What this means is different depending on which company you listen to, but basically it means using the Internet (or cloud) to give you access to your information from any Internet-connected computer or electronic device you use.

You see, the problem is this: Many of us now have several electronic devices that we use daily. We have computers at home, and computers at work. We have tablet computers such as an iPad and we have smartphones such as an iPhone. But as the number of devices we use increases, so does the complexity of moving information between them and keeping them all in sync. I want the photo I took on my phone to be on my computer. I want the document I wrote on my computer to be on my iPad. I want the music I downloaded on my iPad to be on my phone. It's driving us crazy! But there is a wonderful solution, and it's called iCloud.

iCloud is a free service from Apple that lets you access your music, photos, calendars, contacts, documents and more, from whatever device you're using. And it's built into all recent Macs, iPads, iPhones, and iPod Touches. You may have already set up iCloud, perhaps without even realising it, as OS X asks you about it when you first switch on a new Mac. But incase you didn't, I'll show you how you can do so now.

First, click on the System Preferences icon in your dock (or in Launchpad if it is not in your dock), then in the window that opens, click the 'iCloud' icon. If you haven't set up iCloud on your Mac already, you will be presented with a window for you to sign in with your Apple ID. This is the same username and password you use for the App Store, the iTunes store and the Apple Online Store. If you don't think you have an Apple ID, you can create one for free by clicking the blue "Create an Apple ID..." link, and following the onscreen instructions. Then, come back to this window, and sign in.

Once you click the 'Sign In' button, you will be presented with two checkboxes to choose which features of iCloud you would like to turn on. The top checkbox turns on syncing of your contacts, calendars, reminders, notes, and Safari tabs and bookmarks. What that means is that when you make a change on one device, such as changing the phone number for a contact or adding a new appointment to your calendar, that change is also made on your other devices. The bottom checkbox turns on Find My Mac, which allows you to locate your Mac if it is lost or stolen. Tick the checkboxes of the features you want switched on, and click the 'Next' button.

If you ticked the checkbox to enable Find My Mac, you'll be asked to confirm. This feature sends the location of your Mac to Apple's servers so that if you loose it you can log into a special webpage with your iCloud username and password, and see where it is on a map. If you are comfortable with this information being sent to Apple, click 'Allow'. If not, click 'Not Now'.

iCloud is now switched on. You should see a list of all the features of iCloud, together with checkboxes to allow you to enable or disable each specific feature as you like. The features are as follows:

Mail: With your iCloud account, you also get a free email address which is the same as the username you used to log into iCloud. Ticking the checkbox for Mail enables this email address to be used in the Mail app on your Mac. You can find the Mail app in your dock or in Launchpad.

Contacts: Ticking this checkbox allows your contacts stored in the Contacts app to be synchronised across your devices.

Calendars & Reminders: Ticking this checkbox allows your calendar entries and reminders stored in the Calendar and Reminders apps to be synchronised across your devices.

Notes: Ticking this checkbox allows your notes stored in the Notes app to be synchronised across your devices.

Safari: Ticking this checkbox allows your Safari website bookmarks to be synchronised across your devices, and allows websites currently open on one device to be quickly opened on another.

Photo Stream: Ticking this checkbox allows the last 1,000 photos taken on your iPhone, iPod Touch or iPad, or uploaded to your Mac, to be accessible from all your devices.

Documents & Data: Ticking this checkbox allows documents created on one device to be accessible from all your devices, and kept in sync. For instance a text document created on your Mac in the Pages app would be instantly available to continue writing where you left off in the Pages app on your iPad.

Back to My Mac: Ticking this checkbox allows you to control your Mac remotely over the Internet from another Mac, as long as both are signed in to your iCloud account, switched on, and connected to the Internet.

Find My Mac: Ticking this checkbox allows you to locate your Mac on a map if it is lost or stolen, and remotely lock it or even erase it's stored files to keep your information from falling into the wrong hands.

iCloud is seamlessly integrated into many apps, and the number increases daily. You can 'set it and forget it', and your content will go where you go, automatically and effortlessly. It is well worth enabling on all of your computers and mobile devices.

Using Versions

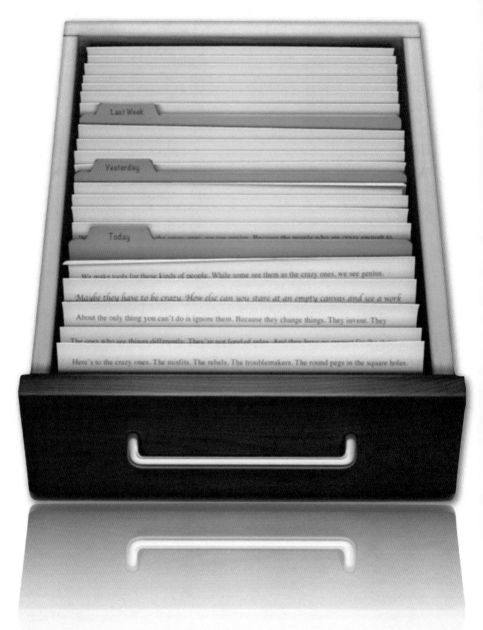

Have you ever wished you could reverse a change you made to a piece of work, but couldn't because you already saved it? Or wanted to get back a part of a document, but couldn't because you long since deleted it? It can be very frustrating to have to manually recreate what you want from scratch, but that frustration is a thing of the past with a feature of OS X, called Versions.

With applications that support Versions, such as Apple's iWork Suite (and soon Microsoft Office for Mac), you can go through the history of changes to your work, find the piece of your document that you lost, and bring it back to the present document. It's not just text documents either, many types of apps for creating many types of work support Versions. It's super easy, and it's quite fun too!

Say, for instance, that one day you open the piece of work you have been preparing for many weeks, and find that somehow you have accidentally deleted one of the sections you wrote last week. If the application you are creating your work in supports Versions, there's no need to worry. At the top of the application window is the title of the file; if you move your mouse cursor over the title, after a second or so a small arrow appears to the right of it. Clicking the arrow presents a drop-down menu, at the bottom of which is the option to 'Browse All Versions...'.

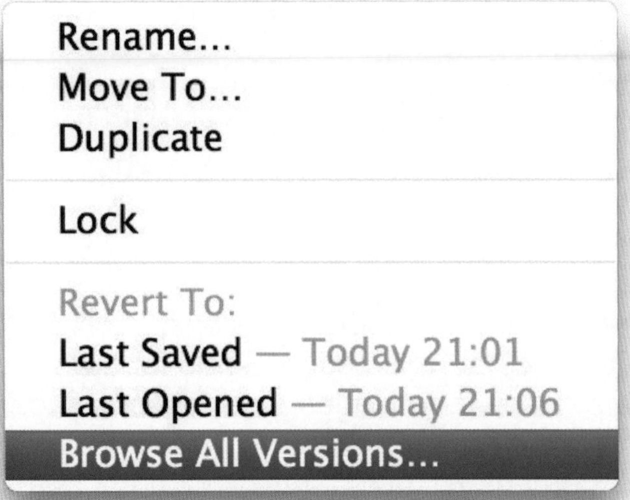

Rename...
Move To...
Duplicate

Lock

Revert To:
Last Saved — Today 21:01
Last Opened — Today 21:06
Browse All Versions...

With a click of the option, the normal desktop interface slides away to reveal a nebula in space, complete with stars flying past the screen. The work you are preparing is shown on the left, and to the right of it is a cascading history of 'snapshots' showing the changes you have made over time, together with a timeline on the far right edge of the screen going from the date you first saved the work to the last time it was saved. By hovering your cursor over this timeline, the exact date and time of each snapshot is shown. Suppose you know for certain that the section you have accidentally deleted was still there two days ago - you simply need to select the closest appropriate date and time from the timeline!

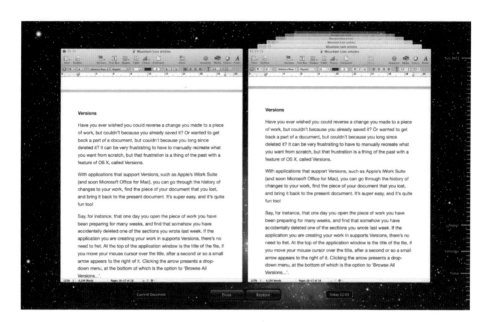

The cascading history of your work will fly through to the correct snapshot in time. Clicking on the snapshot expands it into a full window, and you are able to use the app just as you would normally. If you want to simply revert your work back to the state it was in at the date and time of the snapshot, and remove any changes you've made since, you can press the 'Restore' button at the bottom of the screen. The snapshot will fly back onto your desktop, and you can carry on working from where you were on that date.

More likely, however, you don't want to loose the changes you have made in the last few days, and simply want to bring back the section you accidentally deleted. For this, all you have to do is copy the section from the snapshot back into the current document. To do this, first make sure the snapshot is expanded as a full window, then select the section you want to copy, right-click on the selected portion, and choose 'Copy'. You can then simply click on your current document to expand it into a full window, and paste in the copied section by right-clicking on the area you want the work to go, and choosing 'Paste'. Finally, pressing the 'Done' button at the bottom of the screen takes you back to your desktop, and you can continue working where you left off.

Backing Up your Mac

In the last section we looked at Versions, a feature of OS X that allows us to bring back part of a document from the past. But what if, rather than loosing a part of a document, you lost the entire document file? How can you use Versions if there's no file to use it on? You can't, but you can use Versions' big brother, Time Machine, a backup tool that comes with every Mac.

Time Machine automatically maintains an hourly backup of your entire Mac, including your documents, apps, preferences, and even OS X itself. What this means is a copy of everything on your Mac is made, and kept in a safe place. This way if you loose anything, no matter what it is, you can bring it back again.

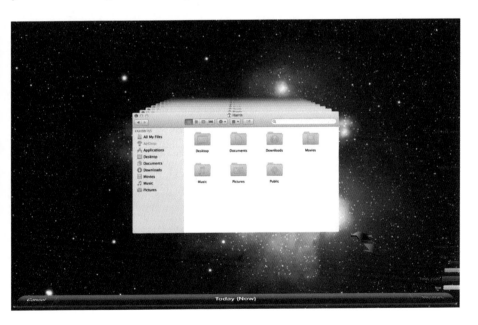

Just like Versions, Time Machine also keeps a history of your files as they change, so should you need to restore a file from the backup, you can choose which date you would like to bring it back from. This also allows you to reverse any unwanted changes you may make to files.

The simplest way to use Time Machine is with an external hard drive. This is a device that plugs into your Mac, and stores files.

Hard drives come in many different storage capacities, measured in GB (Gigabytes) or TB (Terabytes). 1 TB is equal to 1000 GB. As we want to backup all the files on your Mac, you'll want an external hard drive with at least the same capacity as your Mac itself has. Most modern Macs come with between 500 GB and 700 GB of storage capacity. To know for sure how much yours has, check the box it came in.

The bigger the capacity the better though, as the more space your drive has, the more versions of changed files can be kept. Don't worry too much about it getting full from these hourly backups though - Time Machine is very efficient in the way it stores your backups, and will automatically delete the oldest backup versions when it eventually runs out of space. You should be able to buy an external hard drive from the same shop that sold you your Mac, or directly from Apple by tapping here.

Once you have an external hard drive, plug it into your Mac. The first time you connect any external hard drive to your Mac, you should be presented with a message asking "Do you want to use [the external drive] to back up with Time Machine?". Simply click 'Use as Backup Disk' to start using the drive for backups.

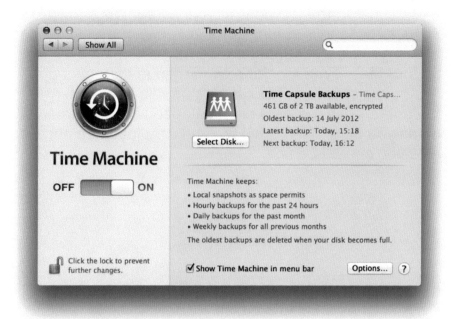

Next, System Preferences will open, with settings for Time Machine. If you want to change any settings, such as excluding certain items from being backed up, click the 'Options' button. Otherwise, simply close the window, and you're done! Time Machine is setup, and backing up.

It may take some time for Time Machine to finish the initial backup of your Mac. You can leave it on to complete the backup, or turn off your Mac when your not using it as you normally do and Time Machine will pick up where it left off next time you switch your Mac on. After the initial backup has completed, future backups should just take a couple of minutes each time.

You can tell when Time Machine is currently making a backup of your Mac by looking at the Time Machine icon in the menu bar in the top right of your screen (as shown below). If the icon is spinning, a backup is currently taking place. If you always keep the external hard drive plugged into your Mac, Time Machine will continue to back it up every hour. However, if you use a portable Mac, you may not want to keep the hard drive plugged in all the time. As long as you plug in the drive regularly, for instance once a week, you should be fine.

Time Machine can also be used wirelessly, without the need for an external hard drive, by use of a device from Apple called a Time Capsule (available here). This device has a built-in hard drive, which Time Machine wirelessly backs up to. Using a Time Capsule is a little too complicated to cover here however; if you'd like to use one I'd recommend making a free appointment at an Apple Store and asking an Apple Genius to help you set it up.

So, what if you should need to restore something from the backup? You can use Time Machine to restore files from the Finder (accessed by clicking the icon of a smiling face in your dock), as well as files saved within apps themselves. Even some apps that have no obvious files, such as the Contacts app, can have their entries restored using Time Machine.

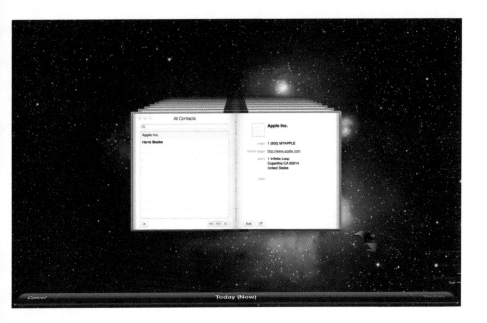

First, open the exact location where the file you want to restore was saved, whether it be a Finder folder, or within an app. Next, click the Launchpad icon in your dock, and click the Time Machine icon from inside Launchpad (by default it's on the first page of apps in a folder called "Other"). Just as with Versions, the desktop will slide away to reveal a nebula in space, complete with stars flying past the screen. The current state of the location you saved your file is shown in the centre of the screen. Behind this is a cascading history of 'snapshots' showing the changes that have been made to its contents over time. A timeline is shown on the far right edge of the screen going from the date of the oldest backup to the current date.

If you know which date you need to go back to, you can click that date on the timeline. Or, if you are unsure which date you need, there are two arrows near the bottom right corner of the screen, the top arrow pointing into the cascade's past, and the other pointing towards the present. Pressing the top arrow will cause the cascade to fly to the first snapshot that is different from the current state of the location where your file was saved. Each click of the arrow takes you further into the past, each time stopping when something has changed. Keep doing this until you get back to the file, folder, or entry that you want to restore.

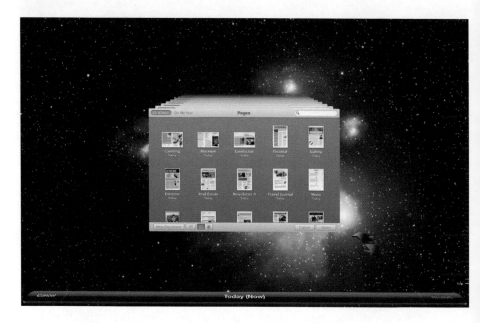

Once you find what you're looking for, click it to select it, and click the 'Restore' button in the bottom right corner of the screen. The selected item will be restored to your Mac.

Time Machine can give you the peace of mind that your information is safe. Although this is one of the more complicated features covered in this book, it is worth taking the time to set up, just in case.

Notification Center

Very often, applications on your Mac need to inform you of things. Perhaps there is a software update waiting for you to download. Maybe you have an upcoming appointment that you have asked the Calendar application to you remind you about. Or you might even have a new message from a friend waiting to be read in the Messages app. These alerts are known as notifications, and OS X has a central place for you to see them.

Notifications pop up in the top right corner of your screen, and then slide off screen to the right after a few seconds. Don't worry if you didn't catch what it said though, it's still waiting for you to read in an area called Notification Center. You can access Notification Center by clicking on the rightmost icon in the menu bar at the top of your screen. If you have a trackpad, you can also invoke Notification Center by swiping left from the right edge of the trackpad with two fingers.

Notification Center will slide onto the right edge of the screen. It lists any Notifications that you have not yet responded to from many apps on your Mac. Examples of possible notifications include upcoming calendar appointments, messages from the Mail and Messages apps, to-dos from the Reminders app, and so on.

If you have a Twitter or Facebook account associated with your Mac, buttons are also shown at the top of Notification Center to "Click to Tweet" and "Click to Post". Simply click on these buttons to start a new tweet or Facebook post directly from Notification Center.

If you'd like finer control over what appears in Notification Center, click on the small gears icon in the bottom right of the screen while Notification Center is open, or open System Preferences and click on the 'Notifications' icon.

Find Any File on your Mac

OS X includes a powerful, efficient and lightning fast search tool, called Spotlight. Spotlight catalogues your computer, and any connected storage such as USB memory cards, allowing you to find any of your files in no time at all.

You can find Spotlight in many places, but the easiest place to get to it is from the menu bar at the top of your screen. On the far right of the menu bar you should see a magnifying glass icon, clicking it opens a small drop-down text field. All you have to do is type what you want to search for.

But what if you can't remember what the file was called? Or even what type of file it was? Here's the magic part — you're not limited to searching by the name of the file. Spotlight is capable of searching inside almost every file on your computer, so that letter you wrote where you spoke about your trip to Scotland...just search for 'Scotland'! As soon as you start typing, you'll see results begin to appear. A drop-down list appears, divided into categories such as Applications, System Preferences, Documents, Folders, Mail Messages, Contacts, Calendar Events, Images, Website Bookmarks, Music and Movies. Right at the top of the list is a 'Top Hit' - the file Spotlight thinks is most likely what you're looking for. Also, if the word you looked for is in the dictionary, you'll see a definition for it, or if you typed a maths calculation the answer to it will appear. Simply click the file you want, and it opens in the appropriate application.

Spotlight can also be found inside all finder windows, and other apps such as iPhoto for searching within those applications' databases.

Type with your Voice

Wouldn't it be good if, instead of having to type out anything and everything that you needed to write, you could simply talk to your Mac and have it do the typing? Now you can, with a feature called Dictation!

Dictation works seamlessly: you say what you want written, your Mac records what you say and that recording is sent to Apple via the Internet. Apple's computers then interpret what you have said through use of sophisticated voice recognition software, and send the written text of what you said back to your Mac. It's incredibly fast, and extremely accurate.

First, you need to enable Dictation. To do this, click the System Preferences icon in your dock (or in Launchpad if it is not in your dock), and in the window that appears click the icon labeled 'Dictation & Speech'. The window will update to show the preferences for Dictation and Speech. Near the top of this window are two buttons labelled 'Dictation' and 'Text to Speech' - click the 'Dictation' button.

vare   Dictation   Time M
ate   & Speech

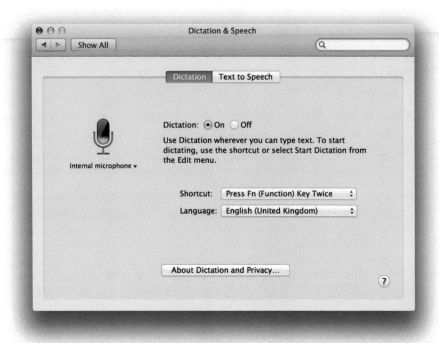

You should see controls like those shown above. First, turn on Dictation by clicking the round radio button labelled 'On', and confirming by clicking 'Enable Dictation' in the message that appears. Second, make sure your language and location is set correctly in the 'Language' drop-down menu. If it is not, click the drop-down menu, and choose the option relevant to you. That's it, you have set up Dictation, and can close the window by clicking the red close button in the top left.

You can dictate text anywhere you can type. Just position your cursor where you want the text to be written as you normally would when typing, and double-press the function key (found in the bottom left corner of your keyboard, labelled 'fn'). You should hear a beep, and a small picture of a microphone will appear onscreen. Say what you want to type clearly, in your normal voice at a normal pace and volume.

ction to the Internet to work.)

You can write punctuation too, simply by saying the kind you would like to be added. For instance, say "Full Stop" or "Period", "Comma", "Question Mark", and so on to insert that punctuation. You can also say "New Line" to insert a carriage return.

When you have finished saying what you want to write, press the function key again. You will hear another beep, and after a few seconds your text should appear! If some of what you said is interpreted wrongly, don't worry - Dictation learns over time, and should become more accurate with each use. In the meantime, simply change any incorrect words by typing with your keyboard.

(Please Note: Dictation requires a connection to the Internet to work.)

Messages

The Messages app allows you to send unlimited free messages to any Mac, iPhone, iPad, or iPod Touch right from your Mac. Messages can include photos, videos, documents and contacts, and are completely encrypted to keep them safe and private.

To get started, click the 'Messages' icon in your dock (or in Launchpad if it is not in your dock). A window will open asking you to sign in with your Apple ID. You will have been asked to set up an Apple ID for iCloud when you first turned on your Mac - use that same username and password here, then click 'Sign In'.

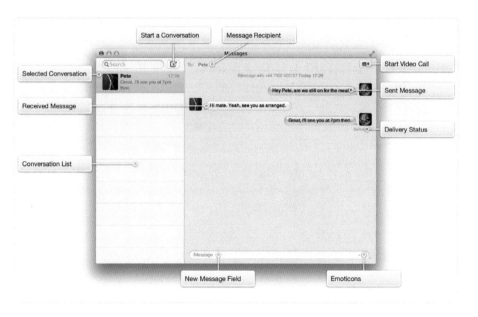

The Messages app is split into two sections: the left hand side shows open conversations, while the right hand side shows the messages sent in the selected conversation. To create a new message, click the button that looks like a pencil in a box, next to the search box in the top left corner of the window.

Next, tell Messages who to send the message to. If the person's details are stored on your Mac in the Contacts app, simply type their name in the 'To:' field at the top of the right hand section of the app. You can also click the '+' button in the top right corner of the window to choose a contact from a list. If the contact has more than one phone number or email address, you will be presented with a list of these to choose which one to send the message to. Contact numbers and emails that you can send messages to will have a blue speech-bubble next to them.

If the person's details are not stored on your Mac, you can type their phone number or email directly into the 'To:' field. Press the enter key, and Messages will check to make sure that contact is able to receive messages. If the address turns blue, all is good. If the address turns red however, that contact cannot receive messages sent from the Message app. Remember, messages can only be sent to users of a Mac, iPad, iPhone, or iPod Touch who have set up their device to accept messages by signing in with their Apple ID.

To start writing your message, click in the text field labelled "iMessage" at the bottom of the right hand section of the window. Then, simply type your message, and press the enter key on your keyboard to send it. Your message will appear in a blue speech-bubble, and you'll see "Delivered" written underneath it once the message has been received.

If you want to send a file, such as a photo, video, document or contact, simply drag the file into the same text field that you used to type your message, and press the enter key once again. You can also start a video conversation with your contact using FaceTime video chat if he or she has a device with a front-facing camera. To do this, click the camera icon to the right of the 'To:' field in the top right corner of the app.

(Please Note: Messages requires a connection to the Internet to work.)

Preview Files, with Quick Look

Quite often I find myself needing to view a file, just quickly, to see what it is. An icon can tell you so much, but sometimes not enough. However, I don't really want to have to open the file, as then I'd need to wait for an application to load up before finding out that it's not the file I wanted. Thankfully, there is another way.

OS X contains a very simple feature called 'Quick Look'. Simply select a file, and press the space bar on your keyboard (or press the gear icon in the finder toolbar, and select "Quick Look..."). Up pops a preview of the file, whether it be a photo, document, music file, video, or whatever; you name it, Quick Look can preview it. Instantly. Then press the space bar again, and the preview disappears. It's very, very useful.

You can also select multiple files at once (by drawing a box around the files you want, or selecting the first file, then the other files whilst holding the command (cmd) key) and use Quick Look to present a 'slideshow' of those files.

When invoked, the transparent Quick Look window appears, with your preview and buttons at the bottom of the window. The buttons change depending on what type of file you're looking at, and how many. The buttons can do things such as go to full-screen, play or pause a media file, view many items in a grid, etc. Hover your cursor over each button to find out its function.

Quick Look can preview practically all of your files because most applications on your Mac 'taught' it how to understand their file type when you installed them. It's a real time saver!

The Mac App Store

Every Mac comes with some brilliant built-in Applications. There's iPhoto for storing, organising, and making things with your photos. There's Garageband for recording and editing your own music. There's even iMovie for editing amazing home movies from your video camera.

But eventually you're going to need more. Maybe you'll want an instant messaging app to talk to your friends abroad, or a word processor to do some college work. Well, there's a one-stop shop waiting for you with all the apps you could ever need: the Mac App Store.

The App Store is a built-in application pre-installed on your Mac. You'll find it in your dock or in Launchpad. Clicking opens the store.

There are five sections to the store:

'**Featured**' shows you the new and noteworthy apps available.

'**Top Charts**' shows you what's currently popular.

'**Categories**' allows you to browse by category.

'**Purchases**' shows you what you've downloaded in the past, so you can re-download for free if you ever need to, and...

'**Updates**' shows any free updates available for you to download for your installed apps.

All applications in the store have been tested by Apple to make sure they are of high quality, do what they say they do, and don't do anything bad (for instance, damage your computer). There are many free apps as well as paid ones, so there's nothing to stop you having an explore!

Keep OS X Up-To-Date

Between your Mac being manufactured and you buying it, updates are likely to have been released by Apple that may do things such as improve performance, increase security, or even add new features and refinements. Updating your Mac frequently ensures you always get the most out of it.

To check for updates, click the Apple logo in the top left corner of your screen, and select 'Software Update' from the drop-down menu (second option down). The App Store will open, with a message informing you that new software is being checked for.

If updates for your particular system have been found, you will see them listed on the screen together with descriptions of what the update is for. Updates for OS X are shown at the top, with updates for installed apps listed below. Next to each update description is an 'Update' button which you can click to install individual updates. However, there is also an 'Update All' button above the updates which will install all the updates in one go. Unless there is an update that you really don't want installed, just click the 'Update All' button. Please note that you may also see the words "Restart Required" in the descriptions for some updates. This means that this update requires your computer to be restarted in order to be installed. Make sure you save any work before continuing with the update if this is the case.

Once you click the 'Update All' button, you will be asked for your password (you must be an administrator to install updates), and possibly to agree to a license agreement or two, before the updates begin downloading. Depending on how fast your connection to the Internet is, together with how big the updates are and how many are needed, this may take some time.

After the updates have downloaded, they will begin to install automatically. Your system will restart if necessary, and you will be able to carry on with whatever you were doing.

Your Mac will check for new updates automatically and even install very important ones by itself in the background, but you can fine tune exactly what it does in System Preferences. Staying up-to-date is a must for every computer user, so make sure to install updates when prompted.

A Simple Way to Change Settings

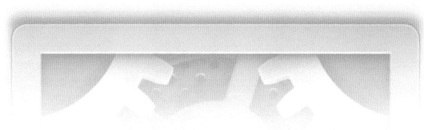

There it is, your shiny new Mac. Its great, but one thing's missing — your normal wallpaper picture. But how do you change it? For that matter, how do you find any setting you want to change? Simple.

First we need to open System Preferences. There may be an icon for it on your dock that looks like a set of gears. If not just click the Apple logo in the top left of your screen, and select System Preferences from the list (fourth one down).

A window will open with about 30 icons in it. Don't feel overwhelmed though, what we want is lurking in the top right corner where you'd barely notice it — a spotlight search bar. But this search bar doesn't search for files, or even websites...it searches for settings.

Going back to our example at the beginning, lets say we search for wallpaper. Unfortunately, we don't realise that on a Mac the picture on your desktop is not called wallpaper, but fear not, OS X knows what you mean, and displays one result: Desktop Background. It also helpfully shines a spotlight on the icon that the setting is located inside. We press the enter key, or click on the spotlit result, and we are taken straight to the setting we needed!

You can also search for settings directly from the main Spotlight search field, located in the top right of your screen (a magnifying glass icon). Both methods work for every setting in OS X, whether you want to create a new user account, setup parental controls, or add a new email account. Easy!

Glossary

Account
OS X is capable of allowing multiple users to each have their own personalised area, called an account. Each account has a user's name and a picture associated with it, allowing it to be selected from a list when Your Mac is switched on. The account holds that user's files and preferences, and can be set up in a way that suits that particular person without affecting the other users of the Mac.

Administrator
A computer user that has an account with higher privileges than normal users. An Administrator can perform tasks on a Mac that others do not have access to, such as update the computer's Operation System, and install new software.

App
Short for Application, a program that runs on a computer, a piece of software programmed to perform a task.

App Store
A place to buy and download Mac Applications, and to update Applications that are currently installed.

Apple Button
The button in the top left of the screen with a picture of the Apple Logo. The Apple button contains a drop-down menu with such common features as Software Update, System Preferences, and Log Out.

Apple ID
The username and password you use for iCloud, the App Store, the iTunes store and the Apple Online Store.

Apple Online Store
The online storefront at www.apple.com/store where you can buy Apple products and 3rd party accessories.

Application
A program that runs on a computer, a piece of software programmed to perform a task.

Back to My Mac
Back to My Mac allows you to control your Mac remotely over the Internet from another Mac, as long as both are signed in to your iCloud account, switched on, and connected to the Internet.

Backup
A duplicate copy of information stored on a computer, kept as a precaution incase the original information is lost.

Bookmark
A link to a favourite website in the Safari web browser. Sometimes referred to as a 'Favourite' in other web browsers.

Browse
The act of viewing webpages on the Internet.

Calendar
The built-in Mac OS X Calendar. (Known in previous versions as iCal)

Checkbox
An box that can be ticked to enable a setting, or left blank to leave the setting disabled.

Click
The act of pressing the button on a mouse or trackpad.

Cloud
A word used to refer to the Internet, and Online Storage.

Command Key
The keyboard buttons on the bottom row that say 'cmd' on them. Both buttons work identically.

Contacts
An application on your Mac that lets you store the contact information of people you know, including names, addresses, phone numbers, and email addresses.

Control Key
The keyboard button on the bottom row that says 'ctrl' on it.

Cursor
The on-screen arrow that you use to point with. When you move your mouse, the cursor moves.

Dashboard
An extra area of the desktop which contains widgets for easy access to information.

Dashboard can be invoked by clicking the Mission Control icon in your dock. The far left space at the top is always allocated to Dashboard, simply clicking on it's preview takes you to it. You can also access Dashboard by use of the same Multi-Touch gestures you use to access all other desktop workspaces and full screen apps, swiping to the right with four fingers until you reach the leftmost space.

Delete
To remove something, such as a file, from your Mac.

Desktop
The area on screen that all windows appear on top of. Icons for the hard drive & any inserted disks can be shown here.

Desktop Background
The picture that is shown as the background of the desktop. In some Operating Systems, this is known as the wallpaper.

You can change the desktop background by right-clicking on the desktop, and choosing 'Change Desktop Background...' from the drop down menu.

Dialogue Box
A message from an application shown onscreen in it's own window. This message may be to tell you something, or to ask you a question.

Dictation
The act of speaking the words you want to type, and having them written through the use of voice recognition.

Dock
The long bar of icons that appears at the bottom of the screen, and holds shortcuts to applications, files and folders stored on your Mac.

Double-click
The act of clicking the left mouse button, or the trackpad button, twice in quick succession.

Download
A file that has been transmitted from the Internet onto a local computing device.

Drag
The act of holding the button on a mouse (or trackpad) in, then moving the mouse (or the finger on the trackpad). This can be used to move objects, or make selections.

Drop-down Menu
Drop-down menus hold commands for the current Application.

Facebook
A Social Networking website on the Internet.

Facebook Post
A message uploaded to Facebook.

Facetime
A video chat Application, allowing you to talk for free with friends and family using FaceTime on their Mac, iPhone, iPod touch and iPad.

File
A piece of information stored on a computer, such as a document, video or photo.

Find My Mac
A feature of iCloud that allows you to locate your Mac on a map if it is lost or stolen, and remotely lock it or even erase it's stored files to keep your information from falling into the wrong hands.

Finder
Used for management of all the files and folder on your Mac. In the finder you can move, rename, copy and delete files and folders.

Folder
A folder is a group of files. Folders can also contain other folders.

Force quit
If an application becomes unresponsive, it may need to be forced to quit. Force quitting an application tell the operating system to close the application immediately, without waiting for it to save your work, so should only be used if the app completely unresponsive.

If you need to force quit an app, you can do so by clicking and holding (or right clicking) on it's dock icon, and holding the option key (also known as the alt key) when you click the quit option, changing it to 'force quit'.

Full-screen mode
Many applications have a full-screen mode, allowing the app to exist in its own workspace and take up the entire screen.

To put an application into full-screen, look at the top right corner of it's window. Apps that have a full screen mode have an icon showing two arrows pointing away from each other diagonally in this top right corner. Simply clicking the icon puts the app into full-screen in its own fresh workspace.

Function Key
A key on a Mac keyboard, labeled 'fn'. It is usually found in the bottom left corner of the keyboard.

Garageband
An Apple Application available for the Mac, iPhone and iPad, that allows music to be created, recorded, edited and mixed.

Gesture
A gesture is a special movement performed on a trackpad or mouse that triggers an action by the computer. Gestures can include pinching, rotating two fingers, and swiping in a particular direction with two or more fingers at once.

Hard Drive
This is a device that stores digital files. Hard drives come in many different storage capacities, measured in GB (Gigabytes) or TB (Terabytes). 1 TB is equal to 1000 GB.

Hover
The act of moving a cursor over an item, but without clicking.

iCloud
A free service from Apple that lets you access your music, photos, calendars, contacts, documents and more, from whatever device you're using.

Icon
A visual representation of a file, button, or other interface element.

iMac
A computer model made by Apple.

iMessage
iMessage is a service from Apple that allows you to send unlimited free messages to any Mac, iPhone, iPad, or iPod Touch right from your Mac. Messages can include photos, videos, documents and contacts, and are completely encrypted to keep them safe and private. iMessages are sent from the Messages app on the Mac, iPhone, iPod Touch, and iPad.

iMovie
An application made by Apple that lets you edit home movies.

Install
The act of loading an application onto a computer.

Instant Message
An application that allows tow or more people to type messages to each other over the internet. The messages are usually free to send and receive, and are received instantly.

Interface
The way in which a user interacts with a computer, such as the onscreen controls on the Mac.

Internet
A network of computers spread across the globe. The Internet is used for such purposes as communication via email, instant messaging and video chats, and for the accessing of information on the World Wide Web.

iOS
The Operating System that runs the iPhone, iPod touch and iPad. It is based on OS X. (Previously known as 'iPhone OS')

iPad
Apple's multi-touch tablet computer.

iPhone
Apple's multi-touch mobile phone.

iPhoto
A great Mac application for storing your digital photos, and doing great things with them such as making photo books, cards & calendars.

iPod touch
A product made by Apple. A small handheld touchscreen device similar to the iPhone, but incapable of making phone calls.

iTunes
A Mac application that lets you buy and play music, rip CDs, Sync your iPhone and iPad, download Podcasts, and more.

iTunes Store
An online store, accessed via the iTunes app, that allows the purchasing of Music, Tv Shows, Movies, Books, Ringtones, and other digital media. The store is run by Apple.

iWork
A suite of apps developed by Apple, consisting of Keynote (for creating animated presentations), Pages (a word processing and desktop publishing app), and Numbers (for creating spreadsheets).

Key
A button on a keyboard.

Keyboard
The device that allows you to type letters, numbers, and symbols into a computer.

Launch
To start an application.

Launchpad
Holds all the Applications on your Mac.

License Agreement
A license that has to be agreed to before using most pieces of software. This license is usually shown to users upon the installation of the software, or the first time the app is launched.

Load
To start an application.

Mac
An Apple branded computer that runs the Mac Operating System, OS X.

MacBook
A computer model made by Apple.

Magic Mouse
A multi-touch computer mouse made by Apple.

Magic Trackpad
A multi-touch computer trackpad made by Apple.

Mail
The built-in OS X email client.

Memory Card
A small device that can store information readable by a computer. Memory cards are often used in portable devices, such as Cameras.

Menu Bar
The menu bar holds the drop-down menus and menu bar items. It lives at the top of the screen in OS X.

Menu Bar Items
Icons to access common systemwide features, such as Spotlight Search, Time Machine, Bluetooth, WiFi, and Volume Control. Also contains battery level (on portable Macs) and the current day and time.

Messages
The Messages app allows you to send unlimited free messages to any Mac, iPhone, iPad, or iPod Touch right from your Mac. Messages can include photos, videos, documents and contacts, and are completely encrypted to keep them safe and private. Messages is developed by Apple, part of OS X and iOS, and uses the free iMessage service, also from Apple.

Mission Control
Allows you to manage the Applications and Windows you have open. Also holds the Dashboard, Desktops, and Full-Screen Apps.

Mouse
The device that you move with your hand to move the cursor.

Multi-Touch
A technology allowing computer input with two or more fingers simultaneously. This allows gestures to be used.

Notes
The Notes application is a place to hold any small notes you need to write down, such as notes for a college lecture.

Notification
Very often, applications on a Mac need to inform the user of something, such as available software updates, calendar appointments, or new messages. These alerts are known as notifications.

Notification Center
Notifications from applications are displayed in the Notification Center, accessible by access Notification Center by clicking on the rightmost icon in the menu bar at the top of a Mac's screen.

Operating System
The software that controls most aspects of a computer, and runs the applications you use.

Option
A preference that the user can choose, either from a list or a preferences panel. The option may perform an action, or change the way the computer works to a way more suited for the user.

Option Key
The keyboard buttons on the bottom row that say 'alt' or 'option' on them. Both buttons work identically.

OS
Short for Operating System, the software that controls most aspects of a computer, and runs the applications you use.

OS X
The Operating System that runs the Mac. It is also at the core of iOS. The 'X' is a roman numeral, and is pronounced "Ten". (OS X was previously known as 'Mac OS X'.)

Pages
A page layout and word processing application made by Apple. It is part of the iWork suite of apps.

Peripheral
An accessory which connects to a computer, such as a mouse, keyboard or printer.

Photo Booth
A fun Application, available on the Mac and iPad, for taking photos and videos with the built-in FaceTime camera. Includes fun filters and effects.

Program
Another term for an Application.

Quick Look
A feature of Mac OS X that allows quick previewing of many file types, such as pictures and video.

Quit
To stop and application and close it.

Radio button
A round selection button, like a checkbox, but used when only one item per option may be selected.

Reminders
The Reminders application allows you to create lists of 'to-do's, things that you need to do and want to write down as a reminder. The app can then automatically remind you about an item on your list at a set time, or when you are in a certain location.

Restart
To turn off a computer, and then turn it back on.

Right-click
The process of pressing the button on the right side of a mouse, or tapping with two fingers on a Macbook trackpad. Doing so brings up a contextual menu of options that apply the item that was right-clicked on.

Safari
The built-in OS X web browser.

Save
To store something on the computer as a file.

Scroll
The act of moving across an on-screen item that is too big to fit on the screen all at once. The item can be scrolled to view a different area of it.

Setting
A preference that the user can choose, either from a list or a preferences panel. The option may perform an action, or change the way the computer works to a way more suited for the user.

Shift Key
The keyboard buttons on near the bottom that have an empty outline of an up arrow on them. Both buttons work identically.

Shortcut
A visual representation of a file that is in another location. Clicking a shortcut opens the item the shortcut 'points' to.

Smartphone
A mobile phone capable of running sophisticated software, such as an iPhone.

Software
A collective name for the applications and other programs that run on a computer.

Software Update
A process that allows software on a Mac to be updated. This can be done by clicking the Apple Logo at the top left corner of the screen, and selecting 'Software Update' from the drop-down menu.

Space bar
The large key in the centre of the bottom row on the keyboard. This key types a space in text fields.

Spotlight
File search technology built into Mac OS X, and iOS.

Stack
A group of folders on the dock which 'spring' open for easy access when clicked.

Sync
Short for 'Synchronise', the process of keeping items the same across two or more devices. Therefore, if an item is edited on one device, the edit is 'synced' to all other devices.

Synchronise
The process of keeping items the same across two or more devices. Therefore, if an item is edited on one device, the edit is 'synced' to all other devices.

System Preferences
The place to go to alter your Mac's settings.

Tab
On-screen buttons that change the view of an application to show a different section. For instance, tabs are used in System Preferences to show different sections of settings.

Tablet Computer
A computer with a flat, hand-held form factor akin that of a stone tablet or a book, such as an iPad.

Text field
An area where text can be typed by use of the keyboard.

Thumbnail
A small picture that acts as a preview of a larger image, video, or document. Thumbnails are often used as file icons in the Finder.

Time Capsule
A device from Apple which enables wireless backups on a Mac using Time Machine. This device has a built-in hard drive, which Time Machine wirelessly backs up to, negating the need to plug an external hard drive directly into the Mac.

Time Machine
A backup tool that comes with every Mac. Time Machine automatically maintains an hourly backup of a Mac, including documents, apps, preferences, and even OS X itself.

Toolbar
An area of an application where functions and tools are available to select for use.

Trackpad
A device that allows the cursor to be moved my drawing a finger across it's surface. Trackpads are usually seem on laptops and notebooks as an alternative to the mouse.

Trash
The trash holds files ready to be deleted. Dragging a file to the trash icon on the far right of the dock puts it in the trash, and emptying the trash deletes all the files in it.

Tweet
A message sent over the Twitter service.

Twitter
An Internet company which runs a social networking service allowing users to send messages, or 'tweets', of no more than 140 characters that are usually publicly visible to other users of the service.

Update
The act of downloading a newer version of an app or other software that is installed on a computer.

Versions
Versions is a feature of OS X that allows a user to go back through the history of changes to their work, and recover parts previously deleted or changed.

Wallpaper
The name given to the picture used as the background of the desktop on some Operating Systems. On the Mac, however, this is called the Desktop Background.

Website
A page available to view on the Internet with the use of a Web Browser, such as Safari.

Widget
A small application which runs inside dashboard, and carries out a specific function, such as forecasting the weather. Information to power the widget often comes from the Internet.

WiFi
Short for Wireless Fidelity, the technology used for wireless networking. Also known as 802.11 or Airport.

Window
The framed area of screen where applications are displayed when running. Windows usually have three 'traffic light' buttons in the top left, used for closing, minimising and zooming the window.

Word Processor
An application designed for writing, editing, and formatting text.

Coming Soon

A Simple Guide to the iPad

A Simple Guide to the iPhone

A Simple Guide to the iPod touch

For free simple guides, visit our website at:

www.simpleiguides.com

© 2012 Harris Books

Printed in Great Britain
by Amazon.co.uk, Ltd.,
Marston Gate.